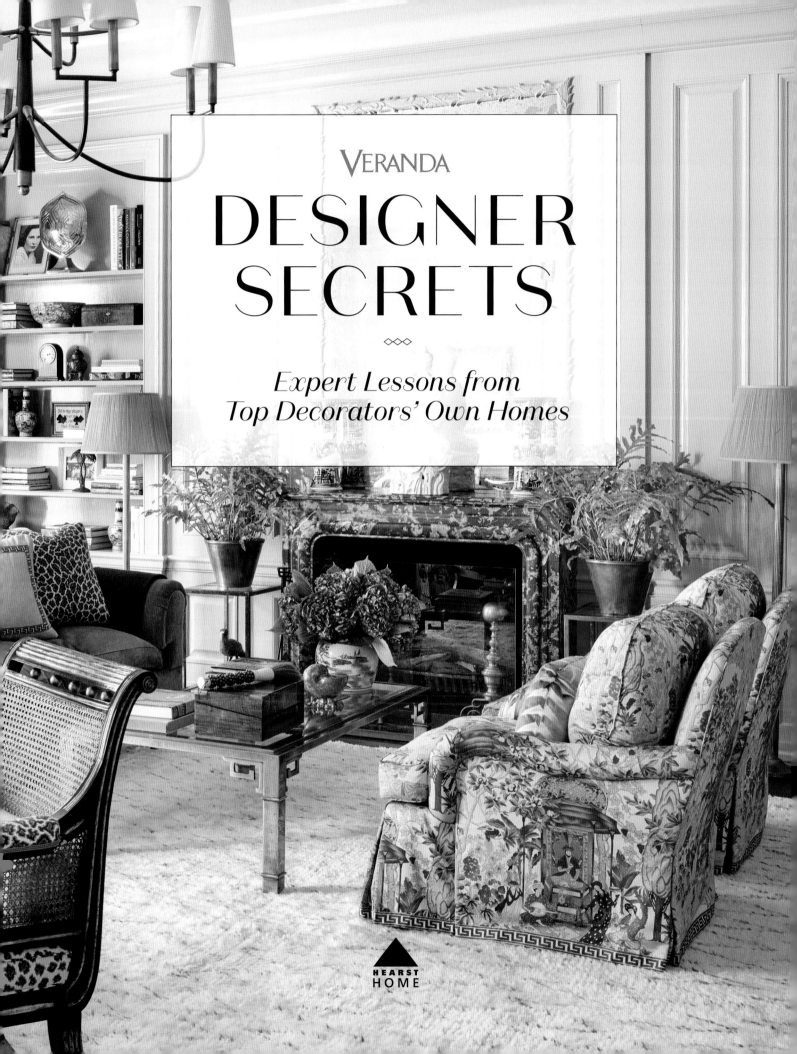

VERANDA
DESIGNER SECRETS

◇◇◇

Expert Lessons from
Top Decorators' Own Homes

HEARST
HOME

CONTENTS

ONE

INVITING
PASSAGEWAYS 10

FOUR

WELCOMING
KITCHENS 80

FIVE

POSH PRIVATE
QUARTERS 100

FOREWORD

Great designers compose so much more than rooms—they are maestros of original style, virtuosos of gracious living, gurus of the good life. At *Veranda*, we're fortunate to call so many of them longtime friends, having cultivated relationships over the years. And we take great pride in being able to share their work, wit, and wisdom with you.

Perhaps most meaningful to us, however, is how so many have welcomed us into their own homes and shared their most valuable secret of all: what home means to them. We have distilled that and so much more here in this collection of designers' private residences. To the designers featured here: thank you for having us—and for inspiring us to live better at home. And to design enthusiasts everywhere: consider this your roadmap not just to a chicer home but a more gracious one where you can embrace true-to-you style. After all, as designer Billy Baldwin famously said: "Nothing you really like is ever out of style."

STEELE THOMAS MARCOUX

◇◇◇

LEFT Working with Sweet Dupuy of Gibbens Dupuy Decoration on her New Orleans primary suite refresh, fine linens designer Jane Scott Hodges fashioned a damask skirt for a side table. It can be drawn up "like a ball gown" to reveal a cache of linens from her collection.

INTRODUCTION

Interior designers are conduits of creativity, channeling the personal style and practical needs of their clients into a physical manifestation that evokes the most profound sense of home. But what happens when a designer becomes the client, taking on the mantle of provisioning their own residence? As designer Charlotte Moss says, "I call every decorator's home their lab"—a place to experiment and play, as well as a living testament to the world they crave just for themselves.

Peeking inside a designer's home is a glimpse into the inner workings of their beautiful minds. The personal spaces of these impactful artists and creators reveal how they live day-to-day, and how their thoughtfully curated surroundings charge their imaginations and calm their spirits. Whether it's a pink, sun-drenched Mexican hideaway for decompressing with friends, a pattern-rich family home in Alabama, or a romantic French apartment rife with personal collections, these interiors and outdoor oases are alive with fresh notions of livable style that are sure to inspire.

◇◇◇

LEFT David Jimenez's 16th-century manor house apartment, a country reprieve from his expat life in Paris, features original ceramic black-and-white tilework in the kitchen and a glimpse of the ancient oaks, fragrant pines, and open fields that blanket the property.

ONE

INVITING PASSAGEWAYS

Hospitable foyers, industrious mudrooms, and captivating corridors brim with intrigue for what's around the corner or up the stairs, setting a powerful tone. Though transitional spaces by nature, these soft landings are anything but a passing thought. Intentionality is woven into each passageway's form and function. They're deliberately crafted and artfully outfitted, beckoning guests to pause and absorb a welcoming and well-edited scene before rounding the corner to further interior enchantment.

◇◇◇

LEFT The sweeping entry of Renvy Graves Pittman's Bel Air estate channels two of her true loves—blue-and-white porcelain and chinoiserie. A Chinese fretwork fresco climbing with jasmine, bougainvillea, and plumbago—all of which grow on the property—ascends the walls.

LEFT "I loved that the home's historic fabric was largely intact—including an original facade that survived the 1861 fire that destroyed much of Charleston," says Ceara Donnelley of her circa-1740 home near Rainbow Row. The entry features painted tumbling-block flooring by artist Stephanie Poe and a 1930s French console.

RIGHT A scenic grisailles mural by Susan Harter sets a pastoral scene in the Gramercy Park entry hall of CeCe Barfield Thompson. An English Regency-style bench and framed sketches supply bursts of sunshine yellow.

"This house has been my laboratory, my studio, and, after many years of tinkering, has become what home truly means to me: a place that cocoons, welcomes, comforts, and delights." —CEARA DONNELLEY

> *"I envisioned us here in the off-season,*
> *and I wanted our place to feel cozy and layered."*
> —VERONICA SWANSON BEARD

On the island of Nantucket, fashion designer Veronica Swanson Beard and local designer Michelle Holland applied a time-worn finish to Beard's not-so-old cottage. They affixed hand-printed muslin wallpaper by artist Kevin Paulsen above beadboard paneling, which they then layered with plaster and rubbed, painted, and glazed for a patinaed look. Main-level floors received an artistic treatment too, with Paulsen painting a checkerboard grid of espresso brown swirls that peek from beneath a richly hued rug.

In a small seaside village in Nova Scotia, Philip Mitchell reverently restored a historic cottage board by board. To celebrate its rich history, Mitchell and his husband inscribed the year the home was built—1795—in the marble floor.

A towering Louis XVI–style gilt mirror, produced in the 1700s when
extravagant ornamentation fell out of favor, greets guests in the
main hall of Meg Braff's Long Island home. Avian prints flank the piece, and below,
a pair of French armchairs in a floral motif frame a John Stefanidis console.

LEFT Despite her own "granny chic" style, Janie Jones's Mountain Brook, Alabama, foyer leans contemporary, thanks to a little nudging from design partner and dear friend Elizabeth Miles. "Elizabeth is the yin to my yang," says Jones. She pushes me to be more edgy." Jones purchased the large painting for her living room, but Miles recognized its rightful place over a sleek, angular console in the entry.

ABOVE Philip Mitchell and husband Mark Narsansky's art collection takes top billing above the cedar stair rail and balusters in their coastal Canadian cottage. The couple is drawn to antique furnishings and collections but revel in adding contemporary art for interest. "It's a way of loosening things up," Mitchell says.

ABOVE A brilliant arrangement of blue-and-white export wows in Caroline Gidiere's marble foyer, where miniature English cream dachshund Buttercup stands sentry. The cast brass lantern and Greek key molding honor Gidiere's affinity for late Georgian and Regency styles.

RIGHT A school of Limoges fish sets find an ideal habitat in Philip Mitchell's servery. "There were so many of these plates made throughout history, so collecting is really about choosing the types of fish you'd like to see," Mitchell says.

LEFT Architect Paul Bates rebuilt the stairs of his Birmingham, Alabama, Tudor home with glamorous curves and topped them with lacquered handrails. Throughout the abode, Bates uses unfinished wood, an homage to his woodworker father. A leather and reed runner leads the way to the drawing room, where favorite tomes top a quartersawn white oak table.

ABOVE Fashion entrepreneur Liz Lange's reimagining of the legendary Grey Gardens estate starts with a wild welcome in the foyer, shepherded by friend and designer Jonathan Adler: punchy blue leopard-print walls and a painting of former inhabitant Little Edie offers an enchanting greeting. Lange restored the original Dutch front door and banisters. "A foyer should be like the intro to a good essay. It should sum up what's to come," says Adler. "This one is a really trippy mix that is a distillation of the many chapters that unfold after the introduction."

A sculptural wooden table and a fringed, texture-rich chandelier
crafted from leaf fibers of the sansevieria plant punctuate the receiving hall of Raúl Cabra
and husband Michael Sledge's Oaxacan "ex-hacienda" (it was formerly a farm).

After sashaying through an allée of palms, visitors to Rossferry, the Barbadian retreat of London-based hotelier Kit Kemp, are welcomed with a wall of warmly hued Breon O'Casey paintings in the entrance hall.

LEFT After years of vacationing in the chic Bahamian enclave of Harbour Island, Matthew Carter and his partner, architect Brent Bruner, took the plunge and purchased a run-down cottage to make their own. The entry is a composition in organic elegance. An antique Italian chandelier illuminates a vintage Eero Saarinen table and an arrangement of coral "sculptures" atop classical sconces.

RIGHT "Mexico feels like pink to me, so I chose a melon-ish, terra-cotta–type shade," says Summer Thornton of the walls of her Sayulita refuge. A slender fountain surrounded by handmade Moroccan tiles anchors the central courtyard.

TWO

CONVIVIAL LIVING SPACES

From low-lit libraries to sophisticated parlors and drawing rooms, these stylish lounges host lively conversation as naturally as they do quiet repose. A clear invitation emanates: to have a seat and be at ease. Gracious seating arrangements decked in comfortable textiles embrace guests, and treasured collections—top-tier art, cherished mementoes, family photos—beguile. Sinking into a deep sofa with friends over cocktails or relishing the solitude of a quiet morning with coffee and a new coffee table book is equally fitting here.

◇◇◇

LEFT Mary Graham's renovated country home in the north of England is brimming with pattern, texture, and frills. In the bright and airy family room addition, painted checkerboard floors form a lively foundation.

To imbue her renovated 1960s-era ranch with 1930s charm, Meg Braff created a large formal gathering room by uniting the original living and dining rooms. A pair of 19th-century chinoiserie silk panels, purchased at Sotheby's a decade ago, are centerpieces that set the tone for the home. "Those panels contain the palette for the whole house—such beautiful blues, corals, ivories, and greens. It feels rich but not heavy to me," she says. Braff installed Belgian marble mantels to impart a "sense of age and authenticity."

"I love using chintzes in places that get a lot of sun. They seem to get better with age." —JULIA AMORY

ABOVE "Our house is a proverbial clubhouse for all our friends," says linens designer Julia Amory of her family's Southampton home in the summertime. "It's big, open, and easy; we love to have people over." Classic floral chintz and a collection of architectural hangings energize soft green ticking on library walls.

RIGHT "This is where we all gravitate," says Meg Braff of her upstairs media room that's equal parts chic and relaxed. The curves of the Katie Ridder wallpaper echo the low-slung silhouette of a pair of upholstered James Mont–style horseshoe chairs, which are "perfect for gaming and movie watching," Braff adds.

"It's a lot to live up to, such a famous house, so the decorating had to be bold and original," says Jonathan Adler, who aided homeowner and fashion entrepreneur Liz Lange in adding a glamorous layer to East Hampton landmark Grey Gardens. In the living room, vintage Mastercraft chairs mingle with an Arbre de Matisse reverse upholstered sofa.

"The heart of this home is the living space," says architect
Ken Pursley of his Charlotte midcentury residence. "The floor-to-ceiling
glass allows a seamless connection to the outdoors and a gracious portal
through which each season can be enjoyed." A similar flow exists inside.
In the living room, a Calacatta marble partition allows conversation to and
from the kitchen without revealing countertop clutter.

A trio of skirted sofas dressed in Colefax and Fowler's Bowood frame the formal seating area of Caroline Gidiere's Mountain Brook, Alabama, living room. The Georgian-style home was inspired by the simple elegance of properties Gidiere admired on childhood trips to Colonial Williamsburg.

ABOVE "This house was built with love from the ground up," says Janie Jones of Hundley Hilton Interiors of her Alabama new build. Inside, rooms delineated by raised archways flow to patios that organically extend gathering spaces. "We wanted great flow but not an open floor plan," Jones adds.

ABOVE Garrow Kedigian's rich citron living room in New York's legendary Carlyle pays homage to the Dorothy Draper-designed lobby, where her signature yellow velvet sofas (since refreshed) still hold court. Black trim mimics the building's iron doors and windows, beloved by the designer.

LEFT An Italian articulating mobile chandelier captivates in Birmingham architect Paul Bates's renovated Tudor-style home. One of his first moves was to paint the vaulted ceiling's "dowdy dark brown" beams in the living room. "It was probably the most important step to freshening things up," he says.

LEFT After residing in her 1920s New York brownstone for 15 years, Charlotte Moss deemed it fit for an update. In the formerly golden-hued library, she applied a deep red fabric to walls, a move that "gave the art a lift." The material nuances of a faux-marbled mantel and antique Italian sconces shine against the bright color.

ABOVE A drawing room in Mary Graham's country home in the north of England is a visual feast, replete with skirted and fringed sofas and table lamps inspired by Imari and Irish styles.

In the library of her family's Jacobian home in northern Lancashire, England, wallpaper designer Mia Reay's Euphoria design—emerald green birds perched atop vines in bloom—climbs the walls alongside a towering, ornately carved fireplace bedecked with blanc de chine figurines.

LEFT Lauren Santo Domingo, the artistic director of powerhouse brand Tiffany Home, has a personal sensibility that parallels that of the luxury behemoth—one that is grounded in classic style but with a markedly modern-looking perspective. In Santo Domingo's light-filled Hamptons living room, a bespoke daybed basks beneath René Magritte's *The Legend of the Centuries*, displayed above a fluted wood column.

ABOVE In fashion designer Veronica Swanson Beard's Nantucket cottage, the study's mélange of gracious seating invites all-season lingering. With local designer Michelle Holland, Swanson Beard paired a skirted linen sofa and vintage Lucite and bamboo chairs with coastal watercolors by Alfred Birdsey, which nod to the island locale without being overly nautical.

ABOVE Varying shades of white paint unify the interiors of Michael DePerno's well-curated Connecticut cottage. Vintage pieces discovered over years of collecting—a sofa by George Smith and an antique armchair—adorn the warm and inviting living room.

ABOVE In Palmer Weiss's living room, a merlot and canary-yellow palette is one of many testaments to her mastery of synthesizing bold pattern and color. A multitude of seating vignettes evokes the intimacy of a salon. "If a friend comes over to have a drink, we'll perch in a little corner together," she says.

"A living room is usually the biggest and best-looking—not to mention the most expensive!—room in any house, and to me that means you should use it most," says CeCe Barfield Thompson. In her New York apartment, nothing is too precious; here, children and dogs live among antiques, including a 19th-century Chinese screen-turned-coffee table and Louis XVI chairs.

"*One of the greatest things that can happen to you in decorating is the spontaneous, serendipitous moment when you stumble onto something. That's the fun part.*"

—CHARLOTTE MOSS

Charlotte Moss's study is her "safe haven." She hung portraits in a gallery-like arrangement, stacked books sky-high, and composed a basket of fabric swatches on her desk that inspires decor decisions.

LEFT A lime-washed pine sectional offers an easygoing place to land in Raúl Cabra's Oaxacan family room, where a collection of clay heads by José Garcia Antonio mix with equine art atop a wooden sofa table.

ABOVE For Laura Kirar, the reimagining of her 17th-century hacienda in Mérida, Mexico, was more gentle restoration than full-blown renovation, thanks to her reverence for the history and soul of the place. In the sala, custom pigmented plaster walls soar and Noguchi paper lanterns float above a marble and limestone coffee table she designed.

Matthew Carter's Bahamian den is alive with imaginative details and intriguing objets. A framed fuchsia parasol provides a bold focal point above a classic George Smith sofa. A duo of upholstered armchairs ornamented with a waterfall of fringe frame a 1970s coconut shell coffee table.

A sunken open-air living room replete with sweeping built-in sectionals welcomes guests at Summer Thornton's Mexican escape, where "you can hear the ocean and feel the sea breeze." Custom coffee tables made from locally sourced parota wood hold up to the coastal location's harsh elements.

THREE

DECADENT DINING ROOMS

Congeniality is queen in these gathering places, where it's easy to imagine the happy chatter and clinking cutlery of an enchanted soiree. Here, comfortable yet elegant furnishings mingle amiably with heirloom place settings, while statement chandeliers sparkle. The art of creating a divine dining room—and one that won't become a corral for old mail instead of memorable meals—hinges on hospitality. These rooms harness that coveted balance between comfort and intrigue that makes everyday meals and dinner parties a joy.

◇◇◇

LEFT Meg Braff sets a timeless tableau in her dining room with an array of antiques, including chinoiserie panels and a Baltic crystal chandelier. Vibrant silk drapes continue the home's lively color story. "I try to be very thoughtful about threading color through the rooms," she says.

LEFT David Jimenez scoured the villages surrounding his French retreat for art and antiques, collecting a mahogany bookcase and quartet of cobalt Louis XVI–style chairs. "My intention from the outset was to create spaces that feel comfortable but that also feel tied to the beauty of France, these villages, to the French joie de vivre," he says.

ABOVE A classic scene unfurls in fashion designer Veronica Swanson Beard's Nantucket dining room, where an expansive gate leg table is surrounded by custom Windsor chairs. An antique Canadian cabinet serves as a stylish repository for Swanson Beard's stockpile of linens and serving ware, including a collection of majolica.

*"It has such a romantic sensibility.
It looks as if it was plucked right out of Kent."*

—WILLIAM EUBANKS

ABOVE Comprising the east side of his light-filled 40-by-25-foot drawing room, William Eubanks's dining area is a testament to the designer's Anglophilia and devotion to quality antiques and rich details. A 19th-century oak draw-leaf table is surrounded by ornate Charles II–style walnut chairs.

RIGHT A paneled wall is an ideal backdrop for books and framed favorites in the cozy dining nook-meets-library of architect Ken Pursley's midcentury Charlotte, North Carolina, home. A tongue-and-groove table made from leftover flooring repeats the vertical motif, and a ladder crafted of an 18th-century roofing truss feels almost sculptural.

Easygoing floral cotton cushions top an assemblage of antique ladderback chairs in Mary Graham's soft pink English breakfast room. The checked rug mimics the painted floor of the adjoining family room (see page 28).

"I used a few simple colors as a starting point [for decor]. Deep greens, dark browns, and a whole lot of white. This combination feels elegantly organic to me." —MATTHEW CARTER

ABOVE A Noguchi paper lantern floats above a Parsons-style table paired with set of rattan armchairs in Matthew Carter's Harbour Island, Bahamas, dining room. Block-print curtains frame the window and mid-20th-century photography ascends the stairs.

RIGHT "In my previous apartments I bought into the 'neutral wall rule,' but in my heart I knew I wanted color," says jewelry designer Emily Satloff. She worked with Katie Ridder to infuse her Manhattan apartment with rich hues reminiscent of the baubles Satloff fashions. In the high-gloss dining room, walls and trim in a pink-cranberry complement reproduction William de Morgan tilework around the hearth and an English Arts and Crafts–inspired rug.

LEFT Janie Jones and design partner Elizabeth Miles outfitted Jones's Mountain Brook dining room with a custom fruitwood table encircled by midcentury Pierre Cardin chairs. A tiered brass fixture echoes the oval table—, set with Herend china (both designers have the same wedding set), scalloped floral placemats, and spring green coupes—that harmonize with the soft pink walls.

ABOVE In Caroline Gidiere's dining room, a wondrous garden scene unfolds, with spring green and sky blue imparting a soothing tone while lively pattern—hand-painted chinoiserie wallpaper and dining chairs upholstered in an energetic floral combination—invigorates the space. A cache of tableware is covertly stored in four closets located behind jib doors.

A velvet wall depicting flint, fossils, and semiprecious stones makes Colette Van Den Thillart's dining room feel like the interior of a geode. The print is derived from an image of a feature wall she crafted for a client with British designer Nicky Haslam. The room is a prime example of the "plush warmth" that highlights her layered, eclectic style.

"I love setting a captivating table; it's like a decorating project in microcosm, with pretty layers and playful details," says CeCe Barfield Thompson. Her eponymous collection of embroidered linens grace the table. An allover ticking stripe cloaks nearly every surface, while a collection of glossy color-block prints refracts light.

ABOVE "A trip to historic Drayton Hall inspired the robin's egg strié," says
Ceara Donnelley of her Charleston, South Carolina, dining room, where Frances Elkins
loop chairs surround a substantial walnut and bronze table.

ABOVE In Litchfield County, Connecticut, Michael DePerno imparted a quiet sophistication to
the dining room of his 1910 cottage. Clean lines unite the space in the form of English Chippendale
chairs and an American Empire table he salvaged from the streets of New York City.

Mark D. Sikes infused the breakfast room of Liz Lange's Grey Gardens with a bevy of blue, from the rattan chairs and curved custom china hutch to the Paul Ferrante chandelier and sky-hued floor. The columnar botanical wallcovering evokes the kitchen garden just beyond the diamond-paned doors.

> *"I got lots of samples, and we just started playing with which stripe worked best next to another stripe."* —JOHN OETGEN

In John Oetgen's Atlanta high-rise, guests have plenty to talk about while seated around the custom dining table with a 19th-century English marble top. The walls display world-class art—including works by Andy Warhol and Sonia Delaunay—against vivid striped wallpapers in varying hues. The effect brings structure to the free-flowing floor plan.

LEFT A series of walnut panels illuminated by artist Andrew Fisher's gilded wall hangings wrap Fisher and Jeffry Weisman's Mexico City dining room, which "feels like a marvelous cabinet," Weisman says. The chandelier—a white gold–gilded coral creation made by Fisher—is suspended over a table with a custom top in blue tigereye from India.

ABOVE Engaging dinner parties are all but guaranteed in the color-drenched dining room of Mary Graham. Claret red accents pop against an olive backdrop like ripe berries against foliage. Graham employed trim on the window seat and drapes from a collection launched with design partner Nicole Salvesen through Sanderson.

An exuberant mural greets visitors in the vaulted West Palm Beach dining room of designer and antiques dealer Lou Marotta. Painted by decorative artist Chuck Fischer, the gazebo design is punctuated with colorful passionflower blossoms, a whimsical scene that marries well with French vintage chairs and a 1930s table topped with Noir Saint Laurent marble.

Like a pair of statement earrings, a couplet of spirited
gold leaf palm chandeliers dazzle above a 16-foot-long dining table
at Summer Thornton's vacation home on Mexico's west coast.

In Oaxaca, agave is king—and a prominent theme in Raúl Cabra's reimagined former farm. In the dining room, the shape of the plant inspired the pattern of the tile floor and its fibers are present in multidimensional lampshades and textiles.

FOUR

WELCOMING KITCHENS

Kitchens are where life happens. These hardworking hubs are practical first and foremost, but the best cookspaces are well-choreographed combinations of convenience, technology, and style with an almost-magnetic pull attracting family and visitors to perch at the kitchen island or pull up a chair at the breakfast table. Whether expansive sculleries with butlers' pantry add-ons or pint-size galleys, these culinary masterpieces will inspire the ardent entertainer as much as the takeout enthusiast.

◇◇◇

LEFT To her kitchen's original, rudimentary design, Veronica Swanson Beard, with the help of Michelle Holland, installed glazed Moroccan tiles on the walls without grout for a raw, pearlescent effect, especially around a slate backsplash.

"There were four species of wood in the house . . . We decided, with our artisan wood installer, to mix them all together. That's why the floors have this beautiful character." —PHILIP MITCHELL

Seafaring style and cottage charm intersect in Philip Mitchell's shoreside kitchen in Chester, Nova Scotia, where lavender bar stools sidle up to a hemlock island, brass boat latches secure white cabinetry, and marine ceiling lights glow. A tufted leather- and acrylic-upholstered banquette is crowned by a pleated pendant shade. Mitchell and husband Mark Narsansky's assemblage of majolica pottery, a collection initiated by Mitchell's grandmother and continued by his mother and the couple, is alluring and practical. "We use all of it regularly. Those tureens and pitchers are frequent serving pieces," says Mitchell.

> *"I suppose I wanted to try to maintain a slightly old-fashioned way of life through my decorating."*
>
> —MARY GRAHAM

LEFT CeCe Barfield Thompson is a proponent of traditional floor plans for busy, modern families, especially where kitchens are concerned. "I can close the kitchen door when we entertain and forget the dishes until tomorrow." In her charming Gramercy Park kitchen, sunlight pours through original steel casement windows.

ABOVE A sage-green custom island is topped with an oak counter across from a backsplash of leafy Italian tiles in Mary Graham's rural home, a former mill house in the north of England.

LEFT A grocery shelf from the 1800s serves as both pantry and display hutch for pottery, glassware, and serving pieces in Raúl Cabra's Mexican hideaway. On the opposite wall, counters made of ayacahuite wood, native to the region, top the work surface.

ABOVE Floors hand-painted with fog-gray accents by artist Willem Racké ground Palmer Weiss's elegant kitchen, a nod to her passion for art and her home's misty San Francisco location.

ABOVE Stainless steel appliances and an island countertop, as well as satin nickel hardware, impart a lightness to the ebony cabinetry in Caroline Gidiere's kitchen. The space's coziness is enhanced by the vivid colors utilized in the adjoining family room, where soft pink and aqua pillows play with the rich oranges of a pleated lampshade and a banquette, beyond.

RIGHT A beloved collection of Wedgwood plates, hidden from the Nazis by artist Mia Reay's grandmother-in-law during World War II, is proudly displayed on open shelves of the family's kitchen in the north of England.

"This allows hosts and guests to maintain full visual and audible connection and marries the functional and social realms that are essential to the success of the space." —KEN PURSLEY

"I call this the 'Japanese Steakhouse' plan," says architect Ken Pursley of his midcentury kitchen's open, plated-steel prep counter that faces the den. Cleanup, meanwhile, takes place in a large working pantry behind a pivot door (right).

In Matthew Carter's airy Harbour Island kitchen, white cabinetry
and vintage wicker pendants intermix with warm wood touches—mahogany
countertops and Abaco pine beams—for a natural and harmonious effect.

The 60 acres of jungle surrounding Laura Kirar's Mexican hacienda are reflected in the kitchen, where a verdant checkerboard motif ascends the backsplash and is echoed in the faux-bois-finished cabinetry.

> *"In character, in manner, in style, in all things, supreme excellence is simplicity."* – MICHAEL DEPERNO

ABOVE "I knew I had to take care of this place and return it to its simple elegance," says Michael DePerno of his restored 1910 Connecticut cottage. Craftsmanship indeed reigns throughout, including in the farmhouse-leaning kitchen, where wooden countertops gleam in the sunlit space alongside an antique Wedgewood stove.

RIGHT Garrow Kedigian, who jokes that "the best thing I make for dinner is reservations!" transfigured his small Manhattan kitchen into more of a sleek bar with black cabinetry, a curving countertop, and brass sheet backsplash.

"It automatically puts you in this fantasy realm," says Summer Thornton of her Sayulita home's vibrant setting amidst jungle-covered mountains and the Pacific Ocean. In the kitchen, a custom palm mural emulates the world outside, imbuing the space with tropical splendor. An embossed tin mirror hangs above a skirted red travertine sink (right).

LEFT A curvaceous kitchen island cradles a robin's egg blue banquette upholstered in performance leather, embracing Janie Jones's family of four into the heart of the home. "This is really where we live," Jones says.

ABOVE The butler's pantry at Liz Lange's reinvigorated Grey Gardens estate features original cabinetry and paneled walls, which Mark D. Sikes enveloped in a deep teal—a recurring color in the home that appears on upholstery, wall coverings, and shutters—and topped with a collection of Wedgwood plates.

FIVE

POSH PRIVATE QUARTERS

Beauty rest feels most attainable in a bedroom that is as soothing to the eye as it is to the soul. With centerpieces that range from soaring canopy beds enveloped in romantic fabric hangings to sumptuous but subdued upholstered headboards, these refuges check all the boxes for stylish serenity. From opulent primary suites to charming children's bedrooms and grand spaces for guests, these well-appointed boudoirs unleash a series of sweet dreams.

◇◇◇

LEFT Bedrooms in Janie Jones's Mountain Brook home, designed with partner Elizabeth Miles, are deliberately diminutive to save space for common areas. In the primary, rosy-pink accents and scalloped linens project an aura of femininity.

Jan Showers's primary bedroom in Dallas is an exercise in restrained drama, with de Gournay's weeping willow wallcovering flanking the custom canopy bed's opulent parrot-green draped interior. A tufted Ultrasuede bench with chunky Lucite legs and a 1940s French dressing table amp up the luxurious suite.

LEFT CeCe Barfield Thompson's young daughters' room is a rose-colored dream. Walls are trimmed in an ascendant floral pattern, romantic hearts adorn the canopied twin bed linens, and blossom-laden fabric envelops a side chair below sweet pastel portraits of the girls.

RIGHT In the bedrooms of her Manhattan brownstone, designer Charlotte Moss leaned into repeating patterns. "It feels luxurious," she says. In her primary bedroom, a lively floral theme marries with the richly draped canopy bed and French antiques—a pair of lamps and a bedside commode. Collections of books housed unexpectedly, atop a diminutive chair upholstered in leopard print, for example, bump up the cozy factor.

"I love beautiful things, but function really does come first. If my husband, daughters, and I can't be nourished by the beauty of a room, what's the point?"

—CECE BARFIELD THOMPSON

CeCe Barfield Thompson designed "a creamy white bedroom as [her] refuge," with a tailored floral bedskirt and sheer curtains. It's a sumptuous but subdued respite from an enthusiastic application of color elsewhere in her New York City apartment.

Linens designer Jane Scott Hodges wrapped her bedroom alcove in 30 yards of Pierre Frey's Mortefontaine fabric, "which had all the hidden subtleties of color that we wanted," she says. The Hollywood Regency bed, procured on Chairish, is a marvelous canvas for showcasing Hodges's impressive collection of embroidered bedding.

Walls of climbing roses ensconce
a guest bedroom in linens designer
Julia Amory's Southampton home.
The canopy bed outfitted in sweet
pink bedding and an antique quilt
add further enchantment.

BELOW On Matthew Carter's first visit to Harbour Island, a midcentury cottage called Chanticleer Hill caught his eye. Nearly two decades later, Carter and his partner Brent Bruner, an architect, made it their own. They embarked on an extensive renovation including transforming the golf-cart garage into a guest cottage, where limed pecky cypress paneling wraps walls in warmth.

ABOVE "I love the look and feel of hand-painted wallpapers, but they are expensive and I couldn't find anything I absolutely loved," says Mia Reay of her entrée to the world of wallpaper design. In her English Jacobean-style home guest bedroom, Reay chose a tobacco-hued iris-patterned wallpaper from her line, inspired by a botanical illustration from the 1600s. The George III tester bed is draped in Estonian linen.

LEFT A jolt of blue from a bamboo and pine screen amplifies the muraled walls and ceiling in designer Laura Kirar's 17th-century Yucatán home. Colorful pasta tiles, made of cement and native to the area, are arranged in an unconventional pattern to impart a modern flair.

RIGHT In David Jimenez's primary bedroom, where a custom nine-foot, ebony-finished canopy bed holds court, emerald green curtains and pleated silk shades atop bedside brass sconces speak to the French apartment's pastoral station. A turret sitting room, replete with a yellow velvet chauffeuse, beckons beyond.

ABOVE Ceara Donnelley's historic Charleston home is "a place of joy and refuge" and "playful experimentation." In the bedroom, a swath of silk brocade that was "love at first sight" enlivens the stately tester bed. A French Bagues-style ship chandelier from the 1960s sails above stripes of undulating fronds that cloak the skirted settee.

BELOW Ken Pursley says his "flat-roofed, midcentury gem . . . needed a little polish, but underneath the grit, it had a rich personality." In the primary bedroom, prayer scripts in Lucite frames hang over the bed and floating side table.

ABOVE A twin bedroom in Mary Graham's English country home is wrapped in florals, from cheery, bouquet-adorned bedskirts to singular blooms applied to bolsters and walls. A quartet of landscapes hang above mustard yellow headboards and a pine Victorian chest.

RIGHT Summer Thornton wanted each bedroom in her vacation house to be special. In the primary, she delivered with a chandelier that floats above the statuesque coral four-poster bed with a headboard upholstered in a vertical stripe, echoed in the wrought-iron chair.

Charlotte Moss fashioned a pair of black lacquered chinoiserie panels into closet doors for an unexpected and artful focal point in the guest quarters of her New York apartment. Regency canopy beds swathed in silk add a sumptuous effect.

> *"This has become a fun, unpredictable place."*
>
> —RAÚL CABRA

A wall hanging made of agave scrub brushes becomes meaningful art in the primary bedroom of Raúl Cabra's Oaxacan home. Furniture, too, is shaped by regional culture, with side tables inspired by portable cookstoves called anafres and a bench based on birthing chairs.

Applying color to his midcentury Bahamas cottage was an exercise in whimsy for Matthew Carter. In the primary bedroom, the sense that something was missing prompted him to paint beams a "lovely, weird green that doesn't exist anywhere else in the room."

When outfitting her family's getaway on Nantucket, fashion designer Veronica Swanson Beard came ready with a stash of finds she'd stored in her "working garage" on Long Island. "We fixed, restored, rewired, and used almost everything," says local designer Michelle Holland, who partnered with Swanson Beard on the project. In the bedroom, an ocean-hued damask reverberates, adorning draperies and the bed pelmet, canopy, and skirt.

SIX

BRILLIANT BATHROOMS

Prim powder rooms, charming guest baths, and luxuriant primary suites are awash in fresh ideas. After all, diminutive spaces seem to elicit some of the most compelling creative moves. If a designer must be restrained by square footage, you can bet their imagination won't be. Case in point: the resplendent parade of washrooms that follows. These innovative baths feature tubs, tile, and finishing touches that only an artist could dream up.

◇◇◇

LEFT Linens designer Jane Scott Hodges, with Sweet Dupuy of Gibbens Dupuy Decoration, bedecked the walls of her New Orleans bath in a custom-milled lattice in homage to the Crescent City's garden rooms. A valance with grosgrain appliqué crowns the Calacatta marble soaking tub.

"Modern or traditional, if something is beautiful, it will always be beautiful; that is my motto." —MIA REAY

ABOVE Inspired by the wallpaper hanging in the primadonna's dressing room in Sweden's Drottningholm Palace theatre, Mia Reay's blossoming climbing vines add whimsy to the primary bath in her north Lancashire family home.

RIGHT In Janie Jones's Alabama home, Sister Parish's Dolly wallpaper envelops the primary bath while a silk and brass wall sconce accents the walls. The curve of the circular window is mimicked in the dressing counter's swooping backsplash, and the stylish skirted stool adds flounce.

"Even large homes have small, quirky spaces . . .
I love the feeling these spaces evoke—character, history,
lack of perfection." —PALMER WEISS

LEFT Ensconced in custom pewter-hued toile de jute curtains and shimmery mosaic tile, David Jimenez's primary bath feels otherworldly. A bespoke alabaster pendant light from Pierrefonds Antiquités and a vintage pedestal sink enhance the romantic effect.

RIGHT In Palmer Weiss's powder room, a corner-mounted sink seems to float amid walls cloaked in a dynamic bamboo and drapery wallpaper by Adelphi Paper Hangings. An antique Spanish gilt mirror punctuates the space.

ABOVE "Green is basically a neutral for me," says linens designer Julia Amory of her home's vivid palette. An upstairs bath in her 1940s Island Colonial in West Palm Beach drips with the hue, applied via a gingham sink skirt, painted paneling, cloister garden-inspired wall motif, and patinated sconces.

RIGHT Fern-patterned wallpaper climbs above mustard-hued paneling and limestone floors in a boot room loo at designer Mary Graham's English countryside home. An ensemble of Italian tiles with an acorn motif forms a miniature backsplash above the pedestal sink, and a duo of floral pleated sconces frames an arched mirror.

LEFT For architect Paul Bates, the inclusion of a round window is his calling card, a motif he infuses into many of his projects. In the marble-floored primary bath of his Birmingham home, the circular opening acts as a night-light, sending "a glow into the hall so we can see our way around."

RIGHT A floriated linen skirt wraps the broad powder room sink in Veronica Swanson Beard's Nantucket escape. A wooden mirror from Nantucket House Antiques appears to undulate like the sea.

ABOVE In Thomas O'Brien and Dan Fink's shingled 1833 schoolhouse-turned-weekend escape in Bellport, New York, the primary bath is simultaneously refreshing—with its serene palette and light-filled interior—and bold, thanks to floor-to-ceiling tile with dramatic veining.

RIGHT Framed botanicals cradle a display shelf sporting coral and blue-and-white pottery in Mary Graham's English countryside home. A wedding sampler hangs above green paneled walls that surround the tub and a skirted slipper chair adds feminine elegance.

LEFT In their renovated historic home on Long Island, Thomas O'Brien and Dan Fink apply cork tiles, which impart a grounding mix of natural color, to devise a texture-rich office bath for Fink.

ABOVE Andrew Fisher and Jeffry Weisman wrapped their Mexico City condominium bath in Thassos Gold marble for an opulent effect. The copper soaking tub and captivating light fixture hem the sumptuous space.

A clawfoot tub draws the eye to an arched nook in Philip Mitchell's renovated waterside home, where he displays a collection of locally crafted stoneware vessels (above) commissioned from local artist Paula MacDonald. "We love that it was made right here in Chester." A trove of crystal scent bottles beneath the dual vanities infuse the space with sparkle.

"We were constantly asking the house what it wanted to be and it told us." —LAURA KIRAR

ABOVE With a chapel on the grounds and an embrace for her property's timeworn bones, an antique limestone baptismal font sink is right at home in Laura Kirar's thoughtfully restored 17th-century residence.

RIGHT A fantastical bath pavilion topped with a gold leaf crown in Kirar's hacienda amps up the intrigue of a guest room, where hues of the whimsical wall mural are echoed in the intricate details of the structure's exterior.

LEFT A bespoke limestone soaking tub in Summer Thornton's primary bath boasts views of the blue-green Pacific and distant hills. Privacy is a curtain pull away, thanks to peach-hued linen draperies.

ABOVE Mary Graham wrapped a powder room at her English country home in an energetic flamestitch. The colorway, devised with her design partner, Nicole Salvesen, makes the small space live large.

SEVEN

GRACIOUS GARDEN ROOMS

Organic extensions of their indoor counterparts, these open-air enclaves harmoniously merge the comforts of home with the beauty of nature. From ebulliently in-bloom borders and glam pool cabanas to waterfront decks and romantic garden patios that practically demand plein air parties, these breezy retreats are transportive in a way that can only be realized in the great outdoors.

◇◇◇

LEFT William Eubanks's 1920s Tudor cottage may be in Memphis, but the designer has accentuated its English influence inside and out. Ivy, fig, and white O'Hara climbing roses envelop the facade while American boxwoods hem the home's border.

"Some people go crazy about not repeating motifs," says linens designer and shop owner Julia Amory. "I like the cohesion it gives." On the veranda of her family's Southampton home, she draws a link to the library (see page 32), which also sports light green stripe upholstery and floral accents.

Just two blocks from the central square in San Miguel de Allende, Mexico, Andrew Fisher and Jeffry Weisman created a wonderland of a courtyard beneath a trio of jacarandas. They constructed a pool lined with gleaming lapis-blue Talavera tile and a soaring stone poolhouse. Crowning the poolhouse is a rooftop cocktail terrace, a prime place to watch the sunset and enjoy a view of la Parroquia de San Miguel Arcángel, the Gothic 17th-century Catholic church.

This Mediterranean revival in the heart of Los Angeles is Renvy Graves Pittman's paradise. The loggia's salmon-hued seating area plays off a pair of Italian faux-marbled obelisks, which frame a 19th-century sunburst mirror. An olive tree shades the poolside dining patio (right), outfitted with a stone table and wrought-iron chairs surrounded by mandarins and kumquat trees laden with fruit.

"I had been dreaming of a tropical house for a long time, always collecting objects and ideas."

—MATTHEW CARTER

To transform the exterior of the once-neglected Bahamian property Matthew Carter shares with his partner, Brent Bruner, the pair applied Chippendale-style railings to the veranda and a dusty pink to the stucco. The veranda sports an inviting seating area, where a sectional is topped with blush-colored pillows and embraced by Areca palm fronds.

LEFT With more than two acres on Barbados's lush west coast, hotelier Kit Kemp has alfresco dining locations in spades, but meals at the antique pine table in her breakfast pavilion, topped with a mud bead chandelier and turquoise ceiling, are hard to surpass.

ABOVE The coral-pink poolhouse on Laura Kirar's Mexican estate appears in step with the property's 17th-century beginnings but is in fact newly built. Casement glass windows are surrounded by a plaster shell embellished with a crosshatch pattern, an architectural detail Kirar discovered amid the ruins of bygone structures on the property.

"I can indulge in vivid, bright colors here—that strong Barbados sunshine just eats color." —KIT KEMP

A cool swimming pool and gazebo—drenched in color, from the flowering vines that climb the structure to the aqua geometric bedspread-turned-tablecloth—boast ocean views.

LEFT A garden party-ready scene is set in linens designer Julia Amory's Southampton backyard. A block-print tablecloth from her collection, which she began when she couldn't find stylish tablecloths for her wedding, is studded with her cherished majolica collection and surrounded by an explosion of limelight hydrangeas in bloom.

ABOVE On a verdant bluff above the Sussex coast, textiles designer Richard Smith's sandstone home is surrounded by a 15-foot wall and a textured mix of thoughtful plantings, including flowers like delphinium, poppies, and nepeta. Vintage Brighton café chairs and a chinoiserie bench make for an ideal venue for afternoon tea.

LEFT Towering slatted doors open to a bluestone patio that accesses the rear entry of Caroline Gidiere's Birmingham-area residence. An aluminum table and chairs set invites repose among topiaries, espaliered fruit trees, and a dahlia garden, all tended by her husband, Stephen. "It's his playground and stress reliever," she says.

RIGHT Behind misty-green folding louvered doors, a poolside bar topped with glazed tile courts thirsty poolgoers at Ceara Donnelley's 18th-century Charleston abode.

Eight dogs, including Dalmatian Mr. James, reside at Raúl Cabra and Michael Sledge's home in Oaxaca, Mexico. In the central corridor, vintage William Spratling tropical wood and leather chairs mingle with the couple's plant collection.

Original Moorish arches flocked by white curtains anchor Laura Kirar's splendid portico in Mérida, Mexico. Grounded by a zigzag pattern composed of four shades of stone flooring, a spirited table surrounded by Mayan Revival dining chairs is set with a color-block tablecloth, handwoven sisal placemats, and antique Oaxacan dinnerware.

Linen designer Julia Amory outfitted her West Palm Beach loggia with fretted seating, including a canopied daybed, and accented the space with large-scale floral throw pillows that blend delightfully with the verdant, palm-fringed surroundings.

"[On the grounds] there's almost a quietness and you feel like you don't even know where you are. It has this strangely magical, peaceful, beautiful atmosphere." —LIZ LANGE

Mark D. Sikes added a touch of Hollywood glam to the circular pool at Grey Gardens. Chic, custom chaise longues featuring individual canopies offer lounge-worthy seating. In the cabana, Sikes commissioned decorative painter Bob Christian to apply blue stripes for a tented effect.

INDEX

NOTE: Page references of photos indicate locations of captions.

◇◇◇

HOME INDEX

◇◇◇

◇◇◇

PAGE 1
Soft pink roses bloom across linen designer Julia Amory's Palm Beach bedroom, where the garden comes alive to trim a skirted dressing table and climb the walls. A pair of column lamps with soft green pleated shades stretch upward alongside an Indian mirror.

PAGES 2-3
Meg Braff approached color head-on in the library of her Locust Valley, Long Island, home, glossing walls in a chartreuse that emphasizes the room's natural light and 1960s paneling. Cane-back armchairs upholstered in leopard-print fabric bring a sense of surprise.

PHOTOGRAPHY CREDITS

◇◇◇

Laurey W. Glenn Cover (Artwork: © 2024 Artists Rights Society [ARS], New York/ADAGP, Paris), 4, 18, 38 (top), 64, 98, 100, 129

Nick Mele 1, 5, 32, 110-111, 132, 148-149, 160, 166-167

Annie Schlechter 2-3, 4, 16, 17, 19, 21, 25, 27, 30, 31, 33, 53, 54, 78, 82, 83, 96, 97, 119, 140, 141, 144, 156, 158, 159

Pascal Chevallier 5, 23, 34, 70-71, 99, 168, 169

Brian Woodcock 5, 36-37, 65, 88, 162, 175

Simon Brown 5, 28, 41, 45, 60-61, 75, 85, 118, 133, 137, 145

Alison Gootee 6, 51, 63, 93, 108-109, 114, 126, 142, 143, 157, 165

Xavier Béjot 8, 56, 115, 130

Pieter Estersohn 10, 152, 153

Brie Williams 12, 20, 26, 52, 62, 69 (top), 92, 112, 116, 123, 154, 155, 163, back cover

Thomas Loof 13, 38 (bottom), 47, 68, 72, 73, 84, 95, 104, 106-107

Ngoc Minh Ngo 14, 15, 57, 80, 124-125, 135

Becky Luigart-Stayner 22, 39, 134

José Margaleff 24, 50, 79, 86, 122, 164

William Abranowicz 35, 59, 90, 91, 117

Miguel Flores-Vianna 40, 48-49, 105, 120-121

Simon Upton 42-43, 89, 113, 128

Noe Dewitt 44

Laura Resen 46 (top), 69 (bottom), 94

Francesco Lagnese 46 (bottom), 87, 131, 136, 138

Melanie Acevedo 58, 146

Max Kim-Bee 66-67

Matthew Millman 74, 139, 150, 151

Björn Wallander 76-77

Victoria Pearson 102-103

Dylan Thomas 161

ABOUT THE AUTHORS

◇◇◇

SUSAN HALL MAHON is a lifestyle journalist and editor covering home, garden, food, health, and travel. She got her start at *Southern Living* magazine after graduating with a journalism degree from the University of North Carolina at Chapel Hill and has held top editorial roles at *Allrecipes.com*, *Coastal Living*, *Myrecipes.com*, and *Health* magazine. She lives in Birmingham, Alabama, where she loves to hike and play outside with her husband, two young daughters, and senior citizen hound dog.

STEELE THOMAS MARCOUX is the editor of VERANDA and a veteran of the design publishing industry, having served in senior editorial roles at *Country Living*, *Coastal Living*, and *Southern Living*. She is a member of the board of directors of the Alabama School of Fine Arts in Birmingham, where she lives with her husband, two sons, and two dogs.

VERANDA

EDITOR-IN-CHIEF: Steele Thomas Marcoux
CREATIVE DIRECTOR: Victor Maze
EXECUTIVE EDITOR: Ellen McGauley
MANAGING EDITOR: Amy Lowe Mitchell
VISUAL DIRECTOR: Kate Phillips
VISUAL EDITOR: Ian Palmer

HEARST HOME
VICE PRESIDENT, PUBLISHER, HEARST BOOKS: Jacqueline Deval
DEPUTY DIRECTOR, HEARST BOOKS: Nicole Fisher
SENIOR PHOTO EDITOR: Cinzia Reale-Castello
DEPUTY MANAGING EDITOR, HEARST BOOKS: Maria Ramroop
SENIOR SALES & MARKETING COORDINATOR: Nicole Plonski
PROJECT EDITOR: Leah Tracosas Jenness
PROJECT WRITER: Susan Hall Mahon
PROJECT ART DIRECTOR: Erynn Hassinger
DIGITAL IMAGE SPECIALIST: Ruth Vazquez
COPY EDITOR: Vanessa Weiman
INDEXER: Jay Krieder
PRODUCTION CONSULTANT: Bill Rose
PREPRESS CONSULTANT: Ray Chokov

PUBLISHED BY HEARST
PRESIDENT & CHIEF EXECUTIVE OFFICER: Steven R. Swartz
CHAIRMAN: William R. Hearst III
EXECUTIVE VICE CHAIRMAN: Frank A. Bennack, Jr.

HEARST MAGAZINE MEDIA INC
PRESIDENT: Debi Chirichella
GENERAL MANAGER, HEARST FASHION & LUXURY GROUP: Alicianne Rand
GLOBAL CHIEF REVENUE OFFICER: Lisa Ryan Howard
EDITORIAL DIRECTOR: Lucy Kaylin
CHIEF FINANCIAL & STRATEGY OFFICER; TREASURER: Regina Buckley
CONSUMER GROWTH OFFICER: Lindsey Horrigan
CHIEF PRODUCT & TECHNOLOGY OFFICER: Daniel Bernard
**PRESIDENT, HEARST MAGAZINES
INTERNATIONAL:** Jonathan Wright
SECRETARY: Catherine A. Bostron
PUBLISHING CONSULTANTS:
Gilbert C. Maurer, Mark F. Miller

HEARST HOME

Library of Congress Cataloging-in-Publication Data available on request

10 9 8 7 6 5 4 3 2 1

Published by Hearst Home, an imprint of Hearst Books/Hearst Communications, Inc.
300 W 57th Street New York, NY 10019

Hearst Home, the Hearst Home logo, and Hearst Books are
registered trademarks of Hearst Communications, Inc.

For information about custom editions, special sales, premium and
corporate purchases: hearst.com/magazines/hearst-books

Printed in China
978-1-958395-60-8

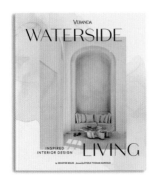
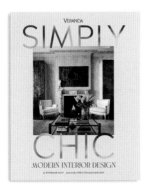